T0146606

Captive Insurance
in Plain English

Captive Insurance in Plain English

F. Hale Stewart, JD. LL.M.

CAPTIVE INSURANCE IN PLAIN ENGLISH

iUniverse books may be ordered through booksellers or by contacting:

iUniverse
1663 Liberty Drive
Bloomington, IN 47403
www.iuniverse.com
1-800-Authors (1-800-288-4677)

ISBN: 978-1-5320-3571-5 (sc)
ISBN: 978-1-5320-3572-2 (e)

Library of Congress Control Number: 2017916089

Print information available on the last page.

iUniverse rev. date: 11/15/2017

CONTENTS

INTRODUCTION

My first book on captives is *US Captive Insurance Law.* It is meant for professionals in the captive insurance industry. It's not for the layperson who wants a basic understanding of what captive insurance is and how it works.

That's where *Captive Insurance in Plain English* comes in. It's deliberately brief; you should be able to read it in one or two sittings. Most importantly, it contains the information you need to make a decision about whether or not you should form a captive insurer for your business.

Before we begin, let me provide a few working definitions and some general background. A captive insurance company – or captive -- is an insurance subsidiary. For example, Acme Manufacturing is a corporation that makes widgets. Acme Manufacturing forms Acme Assurance which sells various types of insurance to Acme Manufacturing. Here's a picture of the transaction:

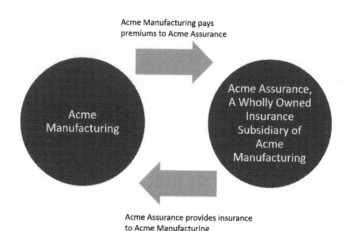

Acme Manufacturing pays premiums to Acme Assurance

Acme Manufacturing

Acme Assurance, A Wholly Owned Insurance Subsidiary of Acme Manufacturing

Acme Assurance provides insurance to Acme Manufacturing

I first encountered captive insurance in graduate school when I read the *UPS* case for a course on offshore financial centers. This decision – that UPS won on appeal -- was the last in a long line of unsuccessful IRS challenges to various captive insurance arrangements. Throughout the litigation, the government argued that various insurance subsidiaries weren't valid insurance companies for tax purposes. The stakes were high: taxpayers had deducted a large amount of premiums they paid to their captives. Had they lost, they would have faced a large back tax bill. Thankfully for us, the IRS lost a large number of these cases starting in the late 1980s; the UPS case was no different.

The decision had a profound impact on me, largely because of my professional background. Before I was a lawyer I was a bond broker where I sold bonds to insurance companies. These companies – when run properly – are very profitable, offering owners a tremendous business opportunity.

In the first chapter, I cover not only the reason why companies started forming captives but also the IRS' unsuccessful attempts to challenge this transaction. This history is vital: it explains both the appropriate business reasons for forming a captive and how to properly structure the transaction. In my second chapter, I explain the legal definition of "insurance" and "insurance company" -- which your captive will have to comply with. The third chapter explains insurance policies -- more specifically, it addresses some of the policies your captive will sell to your company. And finally, chapter four walks through the captive formation and management process so that you'll know what to expect when you're putting your captive together along with working with your captive manager after its formed.

So, let's get started!

CHAPTER 1

A History Lesson or Why Did Companies Start Doing This?

Captive insurance didn't just happen. Negative developments in the insurance markets – such as expensive insurance policies or a complete absence of any insurance coverage for specific risks -- forced companies to form insurance subsidiaries. But the IRS did not believe these were "real" insurers leading to a 30-year conflict between the Service and taxpayers. Although the service had five early victories, they lost most of the remaining cases that had properly structured insurance companies.

It's vitally important to understand this history and the specific reasons why the IRS lost subsequent cases. Taxpayer's victories illustrate structures that are now commonly used in the captive market.

Round One: The Flood Plane Cases

Cincinnati, Ohio, where I was born and raised, is the quintessential Midwestern city. When I was growing up, its population was under 500,000. But its smaller size belied its importance. Cincinnati was not only home to several large S&P 500 companies like Proctor and Gamble, Kroger, and Foleys (which was eventually purchased by Macys), but was also home to a robust service sector.

Cincinnati is also a river city. It started and thrived because of its location on the Ohio River. As in Pittsburgh, St. Louis, Kansas City and New Orleans, river transportation was the city's primary source of business development and expansion. I also vividly remember several times when the Ohio River flooded, causing damage and other problems.

We also have waterways to thank for the first two fact patterns that led to the creation of captive insurance companies. Both Consumer's Oil[1] and Weber Paper[2] owned property located next to a river (the former in New Jersey and the latter in Kansas City). Both rivers flooded in the 1950s, driving commercial carriers out of the insurance market, forcing both companies to form an insurance company to provide flood insurance. **One survived an IRS challenge and the other did not. The histories of these two programs provides a template for what to do and what not to do when setting up a captive program.**

Consumers Oil formed a trust that only sold insurance

---

[1] *Consumers Oil Corp. of Trenton NJ v. United States*, 188 F. Supp. 796 (D.N.J., 1960)

[2] *Weber Paper Co. v. United States*, 204 F.Supp. 394 (W.D. Mo., 1962)

to one entity – Consumers Oil. In contrast, Weber Paper formed an insurance company with other Kansas City companies for the purpose of insuring themselves. The Missouri and Kansas insurance departments formally licensed the insurer in their respective states. Several plan participants applied for and received a Private Letter Ruling from the IRS to make sure the federal government would recognize the transaction as insurance for tax purposes. Despite this apparent inoculation against IRS attack, the Service subsequently challenged the validity of the insurance company – just as they did with Consumer's Oil's trust structure.

The courts ruled Consumers Oil's trust wasn't an insurance company while Weber Paper's was. Key to each decision was the number of insureds. Because the Consumers Oil trust only sold insurance to one insured, the court ruled the trust was an accounting reserve.[3] In contrast, the insurer in the Weber Paper case sold and provided insurance to a group of companies with a similar risk. This larger number of companies insured by the captive helped to create insurance.

---

[3] An accounting reserve is an amount set aside by a taxpayer for a known contingency. For example, at the end of a calendar year, an accountant determines that a client will have to pay $10,000 in federal taxes. The accountant will then create a $10,000 reserve on the liability side of their balance sheet for "federal taxes due." The reserve only applies to one company. In contrast, an insurance company receives payments from a group of different companies. At some point, the insurer receives premiums from a large enough group of potential insureds to become an insurance company for tax purposes.

Round Two: the IRS Wins a Few and
Then Loses More Than a Few

In the early 1960s, the IRS formally announced they would not follow the Weber Paper decision. While this might seem presumptuous (or aggravating, depending on your point of view), it's allowed in a common law system, where anyone may challenge a ruling if they have a "good faith" belief in the validity of their position.

Despite the service's opposition, companies continued to form captives. Some companies' primary line of business was so new they couldn't find competitively priced insurance.[4] Others -were priced out of the insurance markets.[5] Some wanted to write their own policy,[6] while others decided they were better able to manage insurance from within their corporate structure.[7]

Legal developments supported this trend. Starting in the late 1960s, plaintiffs' attorneys started winning large cases using several legal theories: professional liability (especially medical malpractice), product liability,[8] and

---

[4] *Ocean Drilling and Exploration Company v. U.S.*, 988 F.2d 1135, 1138 (Fed. Cir. 1993).

[5] *Humana v. Commissioner*, 88 T.C. 197 (1987) and *Humana v. Commissioner* 881 F. 2d 247 (Sixth Circuit 1989

[6] *Beech Aircraft Corp. v. United States*, 797 F.2d 920 (10th Cir.1986).

[7] *Mobil Oil Corp. v. U.S.*, 8 Cl. Ct. 555, 557 (1985).

[8] The Ford Pinto is the most vivid example. That car's gas tank was very close to the back of the car. If another car rear-ended the Pinto, it had a propensity to explode. Please see this entry from Wikipedia to learn more: https://en.wikipedia.org/wiki/Ford_Pinto

asbestos.[9] Congress inadvertently spurred the trend by passing environmental laws in the 1970s that shifted the liability of toxic clean-up to property owners – a legal shift quickly capitalized on by the plaintiff's bar.

These historical developments had a devastating impact on the insurance industry. Insurers are like any business – their goal is to increase profits. But starting in the late 1970s and continuing into the 1980s, losses mounted. The problem became so pronounced that *Time Magazine* ran an article titled "Sorry, America. Your Insurance Has Been Canceled" on March 24, 1986. The commercial liability insurance crisis that started in the late 1960s and continued through the mid-1980s left companies in a precarious position: they needed insurance but couldn't find it, forcing them to either "go naked" (not having any insurance) or forming a company to insure themselves – a captive.[10]

Offshore domiciles such as Bermuda and the Cayman Islands helped the process by passing legislation allowing companies to form captives. Insurance is an ideal business for small island nations. Insurers required little manpower but brought in a large amount of cash that supported the financial sector. Not to be outdone, some US jurisdictions (Colorado in the early 1970s and Vermont in the latter half

---

[9] For decades, asbestos was used in numerous ways; it was literally everywhere. It also caused lung cancer in hundreds of thousands of people. To learn more, please see this Wikipedia entry: https://en.wikipedia.org/wiki/Asbestos_and_the_law

[10] For more information, please see, *The Tort Policy Working Group on the Causes, Extent and Policy Implications of the Current Crisis in Insurance Availability and Affordability*, February 1986, United States Attorney General

of the decade) passed laws specifically allowing for captive formation.

Despite the legitimate reasons businesses had for forming captives, the IRS continued to challenge these arrangements. But after losing the *Weber* case, the IRS needed a new legal theory for their challenges. They settled on the "economic family" doctrine which no court ever accepted.

The Service proceeded to challenge several captive insurance companies with their new theory, winning their first five cases. A good example is Stearns Rogers whose sole business was designing and manufacturing large power generation plants; that type of business typically required the company to obtain large amounts of insurance for both itself and the client.[11] When Stearns Rogers was unable to procure insurance, it formed a captive names Glendale under the Colorado captive insurance statute. The insurance company was funded with $1,000,000 and wrote insurance for Stearns Rogers, its fifteen subsidiaries, and project customers.[12]

For the purposes of this book, there is one key holding of the IRS victories: **when a captive only insures one company, it is not an insurance company. But when a captive insures many companies, it is an insurance company** The court in *Stearns Rogers* noted the business of insurance involves the "business of insuring others;"[13] **because the captive only insured the parent company, insurance did not exist**. Along the same lines was the

---

[11] *Stearns Rogers* at 834

[12] *Id*

[13] *Stearns-Rogers Corp v. United States*, 577 F.Supp 833, 838 (Col. 1984),

Clougherty court's ruling that **the parent had not shifted the risk of loss to "unrelated parties."**[14] The concurring opinion made the same observation. [15] **This problem harkens back to the primary difference between Weber Paper and Consumers Oil: when an insurer only insures the risk of one company it's an accounting reserve, not an insurer. In contrast, when an insurer provides coverage to multiple insureds (or a large enough company) sufficient distribution exists.**

The Service's victories wouldn't last. Starting with *Crawford*[16] and continuing through *Humana*,[17] they began losing their captive challenges – a trend that would continue until their final early 2000s capitulation in the UPS case. The facts of *Crawford* are illustrative.[18] Crawford made and manufactured valves and fittings. They had four manufacturing plants, four warehouses that stored completed products, and an additional group of exclusive distributors and sales organizations, each of whom purchased insurance from Crawford's captive. **The large number of independent companies buying insurance created risk distribution.** The same situation occurred in *Humana*. By the time of their captive case, Humana had 92 hospitals. The court ruled that due to the large number of

---

[14] *Id*

[15] *Clougherty* at 963 ("Clearly, there is no risk distribution here because there is only one insured and, consequently, there can be no spreading of the risk exposure.")

[16] *Crawford Fitting Co. v. United States*, 606 F.Supp. 136 (N.D. Ohio, 1985)

[17] *Humana v C.I.R.* 881 F.2d 247 (6th Cir. 1989)

[18]

subsidiaries purchasing insurance, the captive had sufficient risk distribution to be considered an insurer.

These facts would play out over the remaining captive cases. As the IRS challenged larger and larger captives, they lost more and more cases because the captives ultimately provided insurance to a large-enough group of companies to be considered insurance for tax purposes.

We've learned two key points from this brief summation of the relevant case law:

Underwriting the parent company's risk must always be the main reason for forming the captive. If a captive is not about risk, do not form it.

The company forming the captive must be either sufficiently large to provide risk distribution from within or it must pool its risk with other companies.

If you'd like a more in-depth discussion of case law, please read my book *US Captive Insurance Law.*

In the next chapter, we'll explore the legal definition of insurance and insurance company.

CHAPTER 2

The Five Factors of Insurance

In this section, I'll explain the five factors all insurance transactions must have, how insurance companies create risk distribution, and two definitions of insurance company. It's very important to understand these ideas because the law requires them to be present in all insurance transactions.

Definite Risk: An insurance company provides compensation when a specific event occurs. The legal term for this is "indemnification," which is the process of making the insured whole. The policy must say, "When "X" happens, the company will pay you money." A clause from an insurance policy might read something like this: "Universal Insurance will indemnify the insured John Dough in the event an asteroid destroys any commercial real estate owned by John Dough physically located in Harris County, Texas." The event must occur before the insurer will provide any funds to the insured, so unless an asteroid hits Houston, John Dough won't get any money. **Fortuity**, or chance, is the second element of insurance. Indemnification only occurs if the insured can't predict when the loss will occur. If planning can mitigate damages, or the risk can be avoided altogether, the insured doesn't need insurance.

A comparison between the accounting concept of depreciation and insurance illustrates the difference. Depreciation is a purely mechanical calculation: if you call your accountant and ask, "How much depreciation does my computer have?" your accountant will be able to give you an answer of "X" dollars. The tax code provides very precise rules to calculate this amount. Compare the idea of depreciation to the asteroid strike from the "definite risk" example: John Dough has absolutely no idea when the asteroid will fall from the sky and destroy his property. Therefore, the asteroid strike is a chance occurrence, or fortuitous.

An Insurable Interest: The third insurance element is an insurable interest—i.e., the existence of a relationship between the insured and the insured property such that any damage to the property will negatively impact the insured's finances.[19] The concept of an insurable interest developed gradually over a significant period and is best illustrated

---

[19] 3 Couch on Ins. § 41:1 ("An "insurable interest" may be defined as any lawful and substantial economic interest in the safety or preservation of the subject of the insurance free from loss, destruction, or pecuniary damage. An insurable interest need not be in the nature of ownership but rather can be any kind of benefit from the thing so insured or any kind of loss that would be suffered by its damage or destruction. Historically, an insurable interest was not a requirement for a contract of insurance"); 1-1 Appleman on Insurance Law & Practice Archive § 1.4 ("The term "insurance contract," as used in this chapter, shall... be deemed to include … a material interest which will be adversely affected (insurable interest) by the happening of such event."

by the life insurance business in the 1800s where people, despite having no familial relationship with an insured person, were able to purchase life insurance on celebrities' lives and thus profit from their eventual death. Courts eventually realized that allowing insurance to be purchased by essentially disinterested parties was nothing more than gambling and was against public policy.[20] Ultimately, the doctrine came to require that the insured demonstrate a strong-enough relationship with the subject of the insurance to justify concluding that damage to that subject would directly hurt the insured.

Risk Shifting and Risk Distribution: Risk shifting and risk distribution were both stated as requirements by

---

[20] Warnock v. Davis, 104 U.S. 775, 779 (1881) ("But in all cases there must be a reasonable ground, founded upon the relations of the parties to each other, either pecuniary or of blood or affinity, to expect some benefit or advantage from the continuance of the life of the assured. Otherwise the contract is a mere wager, by which the party taking the policy is directly interested in the early death of the assured. Such policies have a tendency to create a desire for the event. They are, therefore, independently of any statute on the subject, condemned, as being against public policy."); Hurd v. Doty, 21 L.R.A. 746 (1893) ("The learned counsel for the defendant cites numerous cases to the effect that one procuring insurance upon the life of another cannot recover upon the policy without proving an interest in the life assured. The theory upon which such decisions are based is that such a contract is nothing more than a wagering or gambling contract, and hence is against public policy, and is therefore void.")

the Supreme Court in *Helvering v. LeGierse*.[21] Risk shifting means the insured must transfer some or all of the financial burden of loss to the insurer. This is accomplished via contract – or, in the language of the insurance industry – through a "validly issued insurance policy."[22]

Risk distribution requires a more in-depth explanation, but we already have a good place to start – one of the two conclusions from the preceding chapter: **the company forming the captive must be either sufficiently large to provide risk distribution from within, or must pool its risk with other companies.** In reviewing the cases we learned there was no risk distribution when the captive only provided insurance for a single company. But when the captive sold insurance to a company with a large number of subsidiaries (like in *Humana* or *Crawford Fitting*) or a group of companies (like in *Weber Paper*) there was risk distribution. So, risk distribution is ultimately about the number of companies buying insurance.

---

[21] Helvering v. LeGierse, 312 U.S. 531 (1941) (An insured purchased both an annuity and a life insurance policy very close to her death. After she died, the estate filed an estate tax return and did not include the proceeds of life insurance in the estate. In analyzing the transaction, the court noted: "That life insurance is desirable from an economic and social standpoint as a device to shift and distribute risk of loss from premature death is unquestionable. That these elements of risk-shifting and risk-distributing are essential to a life insurance contract is agreed by courts and commentators." The court simply used the two terms within the same sentence. Subsequent cases over the next 40-50 years would provide guidance as to the exact definition of each term.).

[22] The formation of the relationship between the insurer and the insured along with the interpretation of the insurance policy are governed by contract law.

Most small companies that want to form a captive aren't big enough to have a captive on their own, so they need to pool their risk with others. There are two ways to accomplish this. The first is the fronting model, which looks like this:

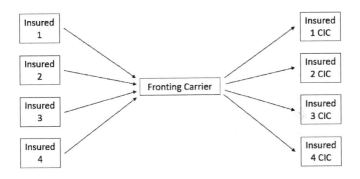

Each captive pays a premium to a single carrier which pools the risk. The fronting carrier then sends money to each respective captive in stages. Usually within the first 30 days after receiving the premium, the fronting carrier sends about 50% of each captive's funds. The carrier holds the remaining monies for 12-18 months to pay claims. If none occur, the carrier sends the remaining money, less a service fee, back to each respective captive.

In contrast, the retrocessional model looks like a hub and spoke system:

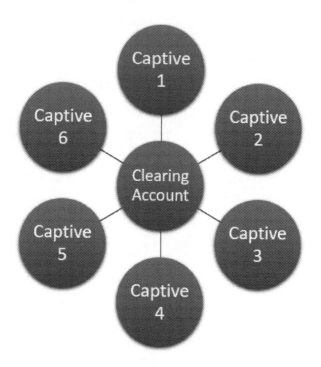

In this model, each captive pays a fee into a clearing account, which then returns funds to the captive (usually within 72 hours), less a fee. Each captive then signs a contract (called a retrocessional agreement) where they agree to pay claims of other pool participants in certain situations.

Claims: Claims aren't specifically mentioned or referenced in any case law. But paying claims, or indemnifying against loss, is central to what insurers do. If you are forming a captive insurance company, expect to pay not only your claims, but, if you participate in a pool, claims for other companies. A good rule of thumb is that every year you should anticipate paying at least 10% of your premiums as claims, for either your company or those of a captive with whom you're pooled.

Now that we've defined "insurance," let's move onto insurance company. We'll look at two definitions. The first comes from the treasury regulations:

> The term insurance company means a company whose **primary and predominant business activity** during the taxable year is the issuing of insurance or annuity contracts or the reinsuring of risks underwritten by insurance companies. Thus, though its name, charter powers, and subjection to State insurance laws are significant in determining the business which a company is authorized and intends to carry on, it is the character of the business actually done in the taxable year which determines whether a company is taxable as an insurance company under the Internal Revenue Code.[23]

Focus on the emboldened phrase, "primary and predominant business activity." Common sense informs us this means at least 50% of the company's gross revenue comes from selling insurance policies to *somebody*. That's it; nothing more complicated than that.

The common law provides a second definition of what constitutes an insurance company called the "Harper Test" because it first appeared in the *Harper* case.[24] Here are the facts the court deemed relevant:

---

[23] Treas. Reg. 801-3(a)(1)

[24] *The Harper Group v. C.I.R.*, 96 T.C. 45, 47 (1991).

1. whether the arrangement involves the existence of an "insurance risk";
2. whether there was both risk-shifting and risk-distribution; and
3. whether the arrangement was for "insurance" in its commonly accepted sense.

Courts have applied this test in several cases, where the following facts were deemed important:

1. The company was organized and operated as an insurer.
2. It was a regulated by a government entity.
3. It had adequate capital (it had enough money to pay claims).
4. An independent actuary determines the premiums.
5. Policies were formed under contract law principles.

A healthy dose of common sense would tell us that these are all things an insurance company does. And to a large extent you're correct. But remember: sometimes the law has to state the blatantly obvious.

You'll obviously need to hire a lawyer when you form your captive so he can provide all this documentation in detail. But now you're able to talk with him as an informed consumer.

Next, we'll learn about insurance policies.

CHAPTER 3

What Kind of Insurance Coverage Does a Captive Insurance Company Provide?

Insurance is a grudge purchase. No one wants to buy it, but people know they need it. So once a year they call an insurance agent, get a quote, buy and receive the policy, and then promptly place it in the lower right-hand drawer of their desk, never to be seen again (until they need to file a claim).

But to understand how a captive insurance company works, you need to gain some fluency in insurance coverage, which is the service your captive will sell to your company. I promise I'll make this as painless as possible! I'll begin by explaining why big insurers only sell certain policies. Then I'll outline some of the more common captive policies, which will complement your commercial coverage.

Insurance companies make a profit when they receive more in policy premiums than they pay in claims. Insurers want claims to be small and, more importantly, predictable. This explains why big insurance companies (like those that are publicly traded) sell insurance for risks they can estimate with a high degree of certainty. For example, if you ask a big property insurer's actuaries--the people who calculate risk and premiums-- how many houses will be struck by lightning in a certain geographic area in a certain year, he or she will give you a fairly accurate number. That's because actuaries have a large amount of data to reference and a long history of losses from which to draw conclusions. But the same actuaries have no idea how many businesses will be investigated by an administrative agency of the government over the same time period (As you'll soon learn, an **administrative actions policy** covers this risk). This explains why big insurers underwrite the former risk and not the later. The former is predictable; the big insurer has a good idea about the size of potential claims, making longer-term financial planning easier. However, the administrative agency risk is unpredictable, which makes longer term planning much harder. Rather than expose their company to that risk, a big insurer simply won't sell the policy.

This also explains how your company can use a captive insurance company. You'll'll continue to purchase commercially available insurance and have your captive provide coverage for risks not covered by the large insurance companies, creating what I refer to as an "insurance tapestry."

Let's look at some of the more common policies issued by captives, starting with a **deductible reimbursement policy**. If your business is like most, you have low deductibles -- usually about $5000. You can raise this amount to $100,000 or $250,000 with your commercial insurer and have your captive sell a "deductible reimbursement policy," which covers losses between $0 and the "attachment level" – the level where the commercial insurer will start paying claims.

Let's next look at a few standard big insurer policy exclusions a captive can cover, beginning with **contractual liability**. Every business signs contracts. But as with all agreements, it's possible one of two events might happen: the other party will breach, or you'll have to breach because it becomes obvious that the other party will not perform his "agreed-to bargain" (This is called anticipatory repudiation). This risk is excluded from all commercial general liability policies; but your captive can "fill the gap." The policy provides funds for legal representation and losses caused by the event.

Pollution coverage is specifically excluded from property policies. It's easy to think that this policy would only apply to a situation like Love Canal – the early 1970s toxic waste dump in New York. But it covers a broader number of situations. For example, pollution coverage would apply to:

1. Removing mold from apartment buildings or cleaning up a meth lab abandoned in an apartment
2. Disposing of waste from hospitals or medical practices
3. Dealing with groundwater contamination of commercial real estate, and
4. Disposing off oil or power steering fluid from auto shops

The obvious common denominator to these fact patterns is that the insured either owns or rents property. A pollution liability policy covers several costs associated with this risk including legal defense fees, errors and omissions on the part of the insured, and cleanup efforts.

Let's now turn to standard captive policies that provide ancillary coverage.

A captive can provide coverage against two risks caused by governmental action. The first is **regulatory change**. The cost of complying with new regulations can be very high. Here are two examples. The *Americans With Disabilities Act* required some buildings to become more accessible to the handicapped. The *Affordable Care Act* – or *"Obamacare"* – required some medical offices to convert paper records into electronic format. A regulatory-change policy helps to defray the cost of complying with a change in the law. In the case of the *ADA* or *ACA*, it would provide funds to either retrofit those buildings or convert paper files to electronic format.

A second policy that provides coverage for governmental action is an **administrative actions policy**. Some statutes delegate interpretive and enforcement powers to an administrative agency. OSHA, the Department of Labor, the SEC and the Federal Trade Commission are just four examples. Each of these agencies has the power to enforce certain laws. The administrative actions policy provides funds to defend against the administrative agencies' action.

It seems as though cyber attacks haven't left the business headlines since the hacking of Target in the winter of 2014. Since then, the Bangladesh Central Bank, several Chicago hospitals, a group of 10 large money-center banks, and a a small group of large health insurance companies have all been victims of some type of cyber-attack. Because of the high costs associated with this liability, it's best to underwrite this risk with a captive using a **cyber-liability policy**.

I went to law school with an attorney who is now a prominent litigator. He jokingly says that you know you're a successful company when you've been sued. While being named a defendant may or may not be a sign of success to some, there is no debate that the larger a company becomes, the more likely it is to be involved in litigation. A **legal liability policy** provides funds in the event of this contingency.

Sometimes businesses are heavily dependent on a single individual for their sales, on a specific business for a large percentage of revenue or a small group of suppliers for business inputs. Thankfully, a captive can provide insurance coverage to defray the risks associated with the negative implications of all three events.

When I was in college, we regularly watched the television show *LA Law*. Leland Mckenzie -- the firm's senior partner -- was portrayed as a wise and knowledgeable attorney with considerable gravitas. He was also the firm''s "rainmaker" - the individual responsible for a large percentage of business. Had he left the firm, it would have lost so much income that it probably would have filed for bankruptcy. To insulate a company from this risk, a captive can sell a **loss of key personnel policy** to the parent, which provides income for a certain amount of time, allowing the company to adjust to the loss of this one key person.

Oil is still king in Houston, Texas, the city where I live. In addition to a large number of major oil companies, the city is also home to a number of small firms that provide professional services to the oil majors. It's not uncommon for a single company to be responsible for 90% of a smaller firm's total revenue. However, if the large company stops hiring the smaller firm, it will quickly go out of business. To help with damages from this loss, a captive can sell a parent company a **loss of key contract policy**, which will provide funds to make up for lost revenue.

Some manufacturing inputs are supplied by a small number of companies. There are a number of reasons for this, but the most common is economies of scale: raw materials require substantial capital investment to develop, forcing companies to eventually consolidate into a small number of large companies. This is called an oligopoly, which has tremendous economic power: they can simply cut off a purchaser's supplies if it is unwilling to play by the oligopoly's terms and conditions.[25] A captive insurance company can sell a parent company **a loss of key supplier policy** to help mitigate the financial losses associated with a supplier cutting off supplies.

My home state of Texas is home to Blue Bell Ice Cream, which is often referred to as the national ice cream of Texas. It's made in Brenham, Texas, where my wife and I had a short honeymoon after our wedding. In the first half of 2015, the company discovered contamination at their manufacturing plant, which forced them to recall their product. This was the big news story of the summer, largely because of the Texas heat. Suffice it to say were many Texans were not happy that summer.

This story perfectly illustrates the risks associated with making a product, the first of which is **product recall**. The Blue Bell story illustrates that any food product can become

---

[25] The OPEC oil embargo of the early 1970s is a great example.

contaminated, causing injury or death. But this risk applies to any company that makes something and sells it; there is always the possibility that for some reason, the company will have to remove the product from store shelves.[26] A captive can provide coverage for this risk.

A second products-related risk is **product liability.** This occurs when there's something wrong with your product that eventually causes some type of harm. The quintessential example was the "exploding Pinto." As you may recall, that car's gas tank was located close enough to the back of the car so that any high-impact collision might cause an explosion. A product liability policy would help any company with a Pinto-like problem pay for damages to people hurt by the product.

Warranty is a third products-related policy sold by some captives. The most common example is a company that sells a product and then guarantees (or "warrants") they will replace it in the event of some kind of defect. A variation of this occurs with contractors, who, for a certain period of time after a project is completed, will repair their work if a problem occurs. A **warranty** provides coverage for this risk

My father was also an attorney. He practiced law with a large Midwestern law firm from the mid-1960s to the mid-1990s. His focus was employment law. He began his career by representing companies in union disputes. By the time he retired, his practice had switched focus to wrongful termination and other employment-related claims. His

---

[26] To get an idea for the breath of the product liability and product recall issue, please see www.recalls.gov, which centralizes the recall orders issued by the 6 primary government agencies tasked with issuing recall orders.

career taught me that employment issues can cost companies a great deal of time, money, and energy.

As a result, there are two employment-related insurance policies that most captives will sell their parent company. The first is **employee fidelity**, which indemnifies the insured for losses caused by two types of theft. The first is low-level shoplifting, which typically occurs at a retail store. The other is for embezzlement which, according to the Society of American Fraud Examiners, can be very costly, time-consuming, and hard to detect[27]. The median claim is $125,000. In 20% of cases, the total loss is over $1,000,000. On average, it takes 18 months to find this loss, which explains why claims can be so high. Because this is a crime of opportunity, pre-employment screening usually won't identify potential perpetrators. An employee fidelity policy provides funds for legal fees related to the loss, restoration of some or all of the losses, and reputational rehabilitation.

A second captive employment-related policy is for **employment law claims**. The typical example is wrongful termination, where an employee will sue an employer after termination. These lawsuits can also be very expensive. They take a little under a year to settle, with the average claim being slightly over $100,000.[28] An employment claims policy will provide coverage for legal fees, and some losses related to the claim.

Let's now turn to risks associated with people, who are covered by workers' compensation and health care

---

[27] https://www.acfe.com/rttn2016/costs.aspx

[28] https://www.hiscox.com/shared-documents/The-2015-Hiscox-Guide-to-Employee-Lawsuits-Employee-charge-trends-across-the-United-States.pdf

insurance. Only medium-sized and larger enterprises can use captives for these coverages. At minimum, a company should have 50 employees and spend at least $200,000 a year for coverage on each policy.

Assuming your company is large enough, using a captive for health care and workers' compensation can lead to substantial savings. But these accrue over time, with the typical pattern looking something like this: in year 1, you'll see a slight reduction in claims, with increases starting in year 2 or 3. This lowers the cost of paying claims, leading to an increase in the captive's surplus, which, by year five, can be substantial. This explains why it is imperative for companies that use captives for worker's compensation and health care to be fully committed to a five-year program.

You must also be 100% committed to lowering the cost of your risk. In the case of health care, you must help your employees lead healthier lives while also enlisting your employees in cost-cutting measures. On the workers' compensation side, workplace safety is a must. If you're unwilling to aggressively reduce your risk, you shouldn't use a captive for these coverages.

These are the most common policies captives issue. In reality, you can write any policy, as long as you can demonstrate two things. First, you must be able to define the risk, which is a key part of the policy-drafting process. Second, you must be able to quantify the risk, meaning an actuary must be able to develop realistic premium amounts for the risk. If a situation meets these two criteria, a policy can be written for a captive.

CHAPTER 4

Welcome to the
Insurance Business!

Now we're ready to discuss who should form a captive, the captive formation process, and provide some general points about running the captive. As with the other sections of the book, it isn't comprehensive; if you want a more in-depth treatment of the subject, please see my book *US Captive Insurance Law.*

In general, I use two criteria to determine which companies should form, own and operate a captive. If the parent company had at least $3,000,000 - $5,000,000 in gross revenue for the last three years, it would be financially advantageous to consider a captive. A second measure is free cash flow—that is, net income plus depreciation. If a potential captive owner had at least $250,000 in free cash flow in the last three years, there are sufficient financial resources to consider a captive. These are the absolute minimum figures.

Captives started as an offshore transaction because this was originally the only place to form one. But starting in the late 1990s, The Internal Revenue Service began looking askance at offshore operations, treating them as inherently suspect. That said, if you already have international operations, consider an offshore jurisdiction.

Let's assume that you don't have international operations and therefore want to form the captive in the United States. With over 30 states to choose from, the choice might seem difficult -- but it's not. First, look for states with at least 7-8 years of experience forming and regulating captives. States that have been in the game this long have the experience to properly vet prospective insurers. Second, look for an industry association, which indicates the captive industry is mature. This is important because if you want to change a service provider, you'll have several professionals to choose from. Third, choose a state you want to visit. A good regulator will want to meet the captive owner at least once every few years. This list of requirements will give you a list of about 7 to 10 U.S. jurisdictions to choose from. After settling on a state, the next step is to form the captive. Let me compare this to forming a non-financial company. There, all you do is sign onto a secretary of state's web site, fill out a form, and pay a fee. That's it. The process takes less than 15 minutes.

Forming an insurance company is a longer and more involved process requiring several professionals. The actuary -- who determines the captive's policies and premiums – is the key figure. I highly recommend using a firm that does business with several captive insurance managers. An actuary who only works for one company is too dependent on one source of revenue and can be pressured to skew his figures. You'll also want a transactional lawyer to organize and structure the program. He or she will also help to draft the insurance policies.

These professionals will write what is referred to as a feasibility study. The name is a holdover from the early days of the captive industry when companies would hire an individual who would determine if the captive was "feasible." Nowadays, captive professionals can tell you if a captive makes sense within the first few phone calls. But, the name lives on.

The feasibility study contains a large amount of information. It will have a menu of insurance coverages and their recommended premiums along with pro forma financial statements for the captive's first five years. A copy of the proposed insurance policies will be included. Each prospective captive owner will also have to fill out an individual application, which amounts to an extensive background check: the regulator will search the credit and legal history of all prospective captive owners. Recent bankruptcies and litigiousness are potential red flags. Regulators also want to know if the perspective captive owner has been convicted of a crime of moral turpitude, such as lying, cheating, and stealing. If you have, don't submit the application.

The process of writing the feasibility study is interactive. The actuary, lawyer, and parent company will trade phone calls and emails discussing the proposed program. The actuary needs extensive information about the parent company's risks and loss history. The lawyer will need a copy of all existing insurance policies to document coverage gaps and corporate documents to properly structure the captive.

After receiving the feasibility study, the state regulator will have additional questions about the proposed program. The process can take as little as 30 days or as long as six months or more.

Once the regulator feels comfortable with the program, he will issue a certificate of authority which grants the captive the legal right to sell insurance to the parent company. Once you have this document, you are formally an insurance executive.

Every captive must file annual reports with state and federal authorities. The annual report filed with the state will include financial statements, an actuarial opinion about the captive's reserves along with an explanation and analysis of all claims. An independent accounting firm will perform an annual audit. The reporting doesn't end there; you'll also file certain information with your federal tax returns, including the amount and number of claims paid by the captive and the amount and terms of any loan advanced by the captive to the parent company. Both reports are usually due in the first half of the year.

You should hold regular meetings with the captive manager and attorney of record to discuss ongoing operations. I recommend you do this at least every six months and preferably every quarter. You should not only take formal meeting minutes but also record the meeting.

A brief explanation of the captive's investment portfolio is in order. Regulators will require that a percentage of the portfolio be held in cash or cash equivalent assets. At minimum, expect this level to be 25%. A majority of the remaining funds should be liquid. Remember: the captive's purpose is to provide funds for a claim. It is imperative that the captive has the ability to convert assets into cash efficiently and at a very low cost. I recommend the bulk of the portfolio be invested in a pool of between 4 to 6 income producing exchange traded funds. The combined beta of these should be less than one, meaning itthey are less risky than the market as a whole. The portfolio should be rebalanced quarterly.

And finally, there are claims. When a risk covered by the captive occurs, the parent company must collect the appropriate data to document the claim, which is then paid by the captive. And, if your captive is using a pool to achieve risk distribution, you'll be asked to pay claims from other pool participants. As I wrote in a previous chapter, expect to pay at least 10% of your premiums in claims annually.

CONCLUSION

First, I'd like to recap the main points that you should take from this book.

1. Underwriting the parent company's risk must always be the main reason for forming the captive. If a captive is not about risk, do not form it.
2. The company forming the captive must be either sufficiently large to provide risk distribution from within or it must pool its risk with other companies.
3. You'll need to comply with an extensive set of legal rules.
4. You'll still purchase third party insurance. Your captive will provide supplemental coverage.
5. You'll need to budget time and resources to manage your captive on an ongoing basis.

Insurance is complex and time-consuming. But if you're willing to put in the time and effort, it can also be very profitable.

I hope you've found the introduction easy to read and understand and, most importantly, informative. If you'd like to learn more about this topic, please see my other book, *U.S. Captive Insurance Law.*

I wish you the best of luck in your future endeavors.

Printed in the United States
By Bookmasters